HOW TO
CREATE A
HOT SELLING
INTERNET
PRODUCT
IN ONE DAY!

By T.J. Rohleder
(A.K.A. America's "Blue Jeans Millionaire")
Founder of the Direct-Response Network

Also by T.J. Rohleder:

TABLE OF CONTENTS

INTRODUCTION

How would you like to have all the money you'll ever need, so you can live the kind of lifestyle you've always dreamed about?

Well, purchasing this book is an excellent step toward accomplishing just that. **If you're willing to study what I'll show you here and put it into practice, I think you'll discover that you got a heck of a deal -- because I'm going to show you dozens of powerful and proven ways that you can make huge profits by creating and marketing your own informational products**. Even better, you'll discover how it's possible to earn massive profits of up to $50,000, $75,000, or even more than a $100,000 a year with information products that you can create in one day or less.

My name is T. J. Rohleder and I'm the cofounder of M.O.R.E., Incorporated in Goessel, Kansas. My company sells thousands of dollars worth of these types of products every day by direct mail and on the Internet and we've been doing it steadily for 20 years. **We've brought in tens of millions of dollars by using the same tips, tricks, and strategies that you'll learn about in this book.** You can potentially generate millions of dollars with this information; I know that because I'm living proof.

All it takes is these secrets, and a generous helping of hard work.

That might sound hard to believe, but when you're done with this book you'll know it's absolutely true. I'm going to show you exactly how you can create these bestselling products and use them to make money for many years to come. No incomplete hints, no come-ons, no pitches for more expensive products; just the unvarnished reality of effective, super-fast product creation and marketing -- guaranteed.

CHAPTER ONE

"Something for Everyone"

In case you were wondering, the process of creating and marketing hot-selling products in just a day or less can work for any business. At M.O.R.E. Inc. we specialize in teaching people how to make money. But you can quickly create a hot information product for any field, leveraging your own knowledge of your industry. That's true if you specialize in electronic marketing, if you're a barber, if you sell books for a living, or if you teach shy guys how to meet women. Before we launch into the meat and potatoes of this method, I want to give you some real-life examples of what I mean, based on real people I know in the marketing field.

Alan R. Bechtold's Story

Let's start with my close friend Alan R. Bechtold, who's literally been creating information products since he was in the fourth grade, when he did his own class newspaper. He's been self-publishing on a regular basis since and has been making money at it since junior high. **The fascinating thing about publishing is that you can literally take something out of thin air -- out of your head or someone else's -- and make money on it.** That's one of the magic keys you're going to learn about in this book. You can produce a product that people want and will pay much more for than the value of the paper it's printed on. You can take a blank sheet of paper that's worth a sixteenth of a cent and turn it into a $50 product. It's that simple. That's the magic of self-publishing.

When Alan discovered electronic publishing and

---

marketing, he just went ballistic; he discovered for the first time that you could actually receive valuable information through a computer that you hadn't paid for or entered yourself. He soon became a pioneer in creating and marketing original information content for electronic bulletin boards. Nowadays, a lot of people don't even know what those were, but they were basically a kind of proto-Internet. They were computer services you dialed up by modem, one computer connecting to another directly over the phone lines. It was quite a bit different from connecting to the huge worldwide network we have today.

In those days, entrepreneurs were just starting to explore how to use bulletin board systems to make money, but they usually lacked the original informational content they needed to attract people. Alan quickly put together a syndicated weekly news magazine that he sold to bulletin board operators around the country. He was one of the very first to do so. The BBS system operators -- or "SysOps" -- made it available to the people who subscribed to their systems. That's when BBS Press Service, the company Alan's still president of today, was born as an electronic publisher. **All it took was one quickly-created, hot-selling product to get him going.**

As the BBS industry grew and people actually started making money at it, Alan's company rolled out a newsletter called SysOp News. It was one of the first true trade journals for operators of online and electronic marketing systems. Later, he moved his company into Web publishing and they're still publishing today. One of their specialties is helping others publish on the Web, which is a fabulous and very effective way of creating and selling products almost instantly.

Don Bice's Story

Another of my friends and colleagues, Don Bice, came

into the market from the banking industry. He cut his teeth with direct mail; he took that knowledge, combined it with his banking know-how, and started doing creative consulting for people in the entertainment and amusement park industries. He used audiovisuals, stage magic, science demonstrations, and animated characters in elaborate presentations for industry giants like Disney and Universal Studios. Along the way, he published some educational material for corporations and really took to publishing. **Like Alan, he learned that it's easy to create something in almost no time and sell it for much more than the cost of materials you used**. That's become a large part of his current business plan, in fact.

One of the big appeals in creating information products is the fact that there's no direct relationship between the cost of production and the selling price. This is something you'll hear me repeat over and over throughout this book. It makes our field unlike those industries dealing with manufactured goods where there are well-established ratios between production cost and price. Always remember this: The value of any information product is based upon its value to the customer. To them, a product's value may lie in what they can learn from it or what pieces they can use and benefit from.

One of the things Don offers, based on his extensive experience, is a single sheet of paper that tells you how to lower your property taxes by two hundred dollars a year. That sheet of paper and the effort he put into it cost him about a nickel -- but the information itself is priceless. **No one's going to question the value of that product**. They may want some assurances that it works, of course; they may want a guarantee, a testimonial, or similar information. But if it works for them, no one's going to say, "Yeah, but you only invested a nickel in that sheet of paper."

See my point here? If you get into manufacturing, then you've got dies, equipment, wages, set-up fees and more, and you can invest thousands of dollars before you ever know whether your product will sell or not. That's not true with printing informational products, especially the type of information products I'm going to be talking about in this book.

They're the kind that require a minor investment of your time and effort, which is exciting because they let you go in new directions, and try new things, without going broke.

Since you might spend roughly a day creating the product, you can afford to take a chance on it in order to see if there's an interest in what you're selling. If there is, you can develop a more elaborate back-end product for even more profit. **Even better, you can operate this type of business anywhere, at any time, and still have a regular income.** This is especially true with the Internet: if you've got a phone and a computer, you can be back in business in hours even if an earthquake or hurricane (God forbid) knocks your house flat. This business offers you an awful lot of freedom.

Jeff Gardner's Story

Let me tell you about another friend, a wunderkind named Jeff Gardner. This young man has spent half his life in the information business -- he stumbled into it as a teenager and just fell in love with it. While most kids his age were asking their parents for money for movies, eating out, pizza, and taking their girlfriends on dates, he was also asking his folks, "Hey, can I have some money to put a camera-ready ad in one of these money-making magazines?"

Well, of course they said "No!" So he had to learn to build his business from scratch, using free advertising -- which is an excellent, inexpensive way to boost your information products.

Nowadays, one of his sidelines is teaching other people how to start their mail-order and self-publishing businesses with free and low-cost advertising. He's leveraged that hard-earned knowledge into a variety of his own information products.

That's part of what's so exciting about self-publishing. **You take something out of your head, something that's simple second nature to you, and you put a twist on it.** Now, we marketers could be very philosophical and say, "Well, I love disseminating information to people. I feel a higher power from giving people knowledge and information," but that's so much self-serving BS, right? I've got to tell you, deep in our hearts it's the cold, hard cash that's important. We like going to the bank and handing these big, fat deposits to the teller and seeing her eyes get as big as dinner plates. The profit margins are incredible.

With that comes the freedom that I talked about in the Introduction. **You have a lot more control over your life, so you can build the lifestyle you want.** I know people right now who are stuck in their jobs with no freedom, no choices, not a lot of control over their lives -- and they're working for minimum wage. If they just had the money that the self-publishing business could give them, they could break through all that and have more satisfying lives.

Recently, Jeff was telling me about a product he created over the course of three or four months. It's only about sixty or seventy pages, but it took a long time to create because he only worked on it a little every day. It seemed to take forever, he said, and you know what? Even after all that, he still had to figure out how to market and sell it. Now, imagine what life is like for people who spend several years on a project they're not sure they can sell.

On the other hand, Jeff once came up an idea for one of

these instant products I'm going to be discussing later on. Instead of dragging it out for months, he said to himself, "Look. This is a product that really can be created in one day."

He had the idea in the morning and created a sixty-minute audiocassette by that evening. That gave him the freedom to immediately jump into the task of writing the sales materials for that product.

Within weeks, orders were pouring in for that product. Jeff sold more than 1,200 of those audiocassettes at $10 a pop. Pretty profitable day, right? **You really can create a product in one day, start selling it fast, have orders start to come in very quickly, and see some profit.** That's the power of this concept. You don't have to spend days and days, weeks, months, and years creating products.

Russ von Hoelscher's Story

Anyone who's ever heard me speak or who's read any of my literature knows that my wife and I owe a great deal to our friend and mentor Russ Von Hoelscher, who was right there at the beginning of our business. He's been creating mail order and self-publishing products like the ones I'm talking about here for more than thirty years. He's marketed literally hundreds of self-publishing products, including books, manuals, and tapes -- and now, of course, he's involved with CD-ROMs, web publishing, and electronic publishing.

But his first self-publishing project, more than 30 years ago, was to write and produce, in just a single day, a booklet called "Mail Order Rackets Exposed." It was only twenty pages long and it turned out to be a good seller for $3 a copy. This little booklet told people how to avoid scams and scamsters in the opportunity marketplace and how to avoid getting in trouble with the postal inspectors. Back then, you could run ads in small mail-order publications for a couple of dollars. He'd often get ten sales per ad per day, which would be $30; but it only cost him a few bucks to place the ad, and a few more to print the booklets, so he made a nice profit.

How did he put this product together in one day?

For many months, he saved articles that appeared in all those little mail-order publications and some of the bigger opportunity publications. People were really on a kick back then, in terms of avoiding mail order scams. All the different scams they were talking about were interesting, so Ross started clipping out those articles. Eventually, he had a big pile of them and he said to himself, "You know, rather than just write an article on this, I could just rewrite, *without plagiarizing*, a booklet or a report that I could call 'Mail Order Rackets Exposed.' And that's how Russ did it. He put it together in one day and then started to market it. That was a very humble start in self-publishing, but he's gone on to much bigger and better things and he's taught a lot of others how to do the same.

Chris Lakey's Story

And then there's Chris Lakey, a very promising young man who works for my company. Like Jeff Gardner, he started out in the field at age 16 -- but he started a bit differently than Jeff did. He needed a job when he was in high school, so he went to work in the shipping department at M.O.R.E. Inc. sending out the mail order products -- the information products and the moneymaking programs that we were producing and selling at the time.

Eventually he got switched to our printing department, and, between those two places, he read a lot of the material we were producing. Over the years he learned a lot and eventually started creating his own mail order information products -- some of them the one-day kind I'll be talking about here -- and selling his expertise. **That's the basis of this process: you're selling your hard-earned knowledge and, by the time you get around to creating your products, it's all so engrained in you that it's easy to create something profitable and useful in next to no time.**

Chris tells me that the thing that excites him the most about creating a hot-selling Internet product in one day is the fact that it's so easy to do, even though you might think that creating a single product in a full year would be tough. You might think there's no way you'd ever be able to create a product in any amount of time, let alone one day. Then, you start to learn how easy it really can be and, of course, the profits can be phenomenal compared to the time it actually takes to create the product. **That's one of the things I love about this business.**

Here's a story I once read in a sales letter that brings to life just how simple it can be to do this kind of thing -- but it also stresses the need to educate yourself in your marketplace first.

When your TV goes on the blink and you need it fixed, you call a repairperson. They come out and take a look at it. Within a couple of minutes, usually, your TV is fixed. You think, "Wow! That's great!" Then they hand you the bill for $75 or $100 and you scream, "Why in the world are you charging me this ridiculous, outrageous price?" The guy looks at you and says, "It's in knowing how to fix TVs."

I think that's a good analogy to the information publishing business. **The value isn't in the amount of time it takes you to create the product, it's in the quality of the information.**

Mark Nolan's Story

Mark Nolan is a student of Russ von Hoelscher who followed his advice and created some quick products. They caught on, and he's been doing it ever since. Learning how easy it is to sell paper and ink, he says, was a cosmic revelation on par with the discovery of gold.

The first thing he sold was this thirty-two page, stapled-together booklet called "*Your Ticket to Free Travel.*" He talked about how to get bumped on the airlines, how to get free rail passes, how to stay at youth hostels for $2. He wrote that little booklet and sold it through classified ads in travel, holiday, and other magazines. That was how he got his feet wet. It took him about a week to type it up on an IBM electric typewriter.

Another way he got an instant product was simply to buy one. He purchased the newsletter Information Edge Marketing Letter, which was founded by Jerry Buchanan, and wham! he was a newsletter publisher. You can start a newsletter yourself; you don't have to buy one. **It's a quick product because you just need one eight-page issue and you're in business. You can make money right away, in just about any field you can think of.** People are selling information on every subject under the sun.

I know a guy who writes a commodity paper. It takes him one day a month to do it. He comes in on a Saturday and writes it in a few hours while it's quiet at his office -- but he makes millions of dollars from this newsletter. He keeps a diary with him during the week to keep track of ideas. You can do the same thing. <u>You can carry around a notepad, or maybe a file or electronic organizer, where you can put your notes and ideas as you have them</u>. Then you can take those pieces and put them together in a newsletter, all in one day. That's how Mark does it and that's how a lot of my colleagues do it. It's fascinating how you can make money from something that happens so fast!

Because, once again: people aren't buying how much time you put into it. They're buying the results and what they can get out of it. That's the secret!

How much can you get paid if you're a chef? You stand over a hot stove. You cook the food. Everybody says that you're the greatest, but you can only make so much per hour.

However, you could create a cookbook by throwing together a collection of recipes you already had in your kitchen one evening instead of watching television. **That book could potentially sell millions of copies.** Even if you make just one dollar per book, you've got a million bucks -- so it's the volume that matters. You can only be in one place at one time when you're the one cooking; but if everybody's watching your video or reading your book, then you can make a fortune.

Mark once told me about an acquaintance, Dee Buss, who did just that. She owns a very popular restaurant where Mark lives, and now she's got a TV show, a cookbook, and a coffee table book. You don't see her at the restaurant much anymore because she's more likely to be off in Tuscany on vacation.

In a similar way, the information business is a great way to leverage your time and energy into something really big. You can do it very, very fast -- which is exactly how my wife Eileen and I got started.

The M.O.R.E. Inc. Story

This business, plain and simply, changed our lives. We got involved in it in 1988, building our company from one publication that we self-published. For years, Eileen ran the whole company and she let me do all the marketing. I got to have all the fun doing the creation while she worked with the accountants and took care of all that complicated managing stuff. She's stepped down since, but I still get to enjoy all the fun of marketing.

Eileen and I started with one thin little brochure; I don't even want to call it a booklet, it was so thin. We sold it for $12.95. I remember the first time one of my relatives saw this book. When we handed it to her, we were so proud of it because we were selling thousands of dollars worth of this little sixteen-page brochure. I still remember so clearly how she looked at it, held it in her hand for a second, then threw it on the floor, and said, "This is crap!" That really hurt my feelings at the time and I spent years being upset with her because of that.

But you know what? In a way, she was right. To the person we wrote our booklet for, it was valuable information. To everyone else, it was crap. **It was just a little cheap brochure, and my relatives couldn't believe that we were selling the thing for $12.95.**

Well, we were. Our customers were very happy. They loved it. People got in their cars and actually drove in from several states away to come meet us after they read it. It was about a moneymaking plan that really, honestly worked, so it was perfect for them. We had tested it, so when people got our little booklet, they were very impressed and excited -- despite the fact that to everyone else, it was just so much crap.

Let me reiterate: the price you charge has nothing to do with what it costs you to create your product. One of the most famous self-publishers of all time was a man named Joe Carbo and Joe made no bones about this fact. He sold one million copies of his little booklet, *The Lazy Man's Way to Riches*, for $10 each, so he grossed over ten million dollars on this one item. Yet right there in his ad he said, "This book only cost me fifty cents to produce, but I'm going to sell it to you for $10." That was a bold statement. He went on to say, "Why are you going to pay $10 for a book that only cost me fifty cents to print? I'll tell you why. This book is going to make you rich!"

I'm excited about writing this book. I can't wait to share some of the ideas we've used to develop hundreds of different informational products over the last twenty years.

You can use the same methods to make all the money you've ever needed.

If that sounds like a good idea to you, turn the page, go to Chapter 2, and I'll start revealing my greatest tips, tricks, and strategies for producing high-profit informational products in just one day -- or even less!

CHAPTER TWO

"Leveraging the Power of the Internet"

Never underestimate the power of the Internet to make you rich because it offers excellent opportunities for the development and marketing of quick informational products. Here's one technique, courtesy of my good friend Alan Bechtold, that will actually take several days for your efforts to come to fruition -- but it only takes a few minutes to plant the seed. You come back, check on what you've planted, and before long you'll have the material for a book to sell.

The key is Internet newsgroups.

If you're unfamiliar with them, they're something like public message boards that are categorized by information category and subject matter. There's one for anything you can think of.

What you want to do is come up with a subject that interests you. This is critical for any information product you ever create: you've got to be interested in it. That doesn't mean you have to know everything about it; in fact, it could be something that's always interested you on an amateur level or even something you'd like to learn about, but never had a chance to.

One of the best ways to create an information product is to gather and document the information as you learn it -- and soon enough you'll be an expert, at least compared to most folks.

Of course, you have to come up with a subject that a

reasonable number of other people are curious about and interested in; it doesn't help to sell an information product to an audience of four.

Since this subject is of interest to you, the first step is very easy. Write down 10-20 questions that you want answered about this subject, items you feel are very important to know. Put it in a questionnaire format and post it as a message in the appropriate newsgroup. In the message, tell people you're writing a book and you need their help. Ask people to answer as many of the questions as they can and to include a couple of sentences with their name, what they do, possibly their email address, and their website if they have one. Tell them you'll be happy to publicize what they do and who they are in response to their help in putting together this information product.

Here's an easy way to participate in newsgroups that works on any computer: **Google Groups**. This is a service that gives you access to read and reply to virtually all of the newsgroups available on the Internet. They're grouped by subject matter, category, and the like, and this makes it very easy to find the right newsgroups for your subject. All you've got to do is set up a user name and a password and you can participate with just a browser. You don't need an email account or anything.

Once you start your research, you may discover that there are several newsgroups that are close enough to your subject matter to cross-post to, so be sure and browse around before you post your questions. Once you've done that, you've gotten the ball rolling -- and you should be able to do it in fifteen or twenty minutes. Give it a week or two and come back and check to see how many people have responded. Another neat thing to do is leave your email address so people can send you more information.

The bottom line is that in a week or two, you'll be

amazed. You end up with enough information to write a complete informational product from a number of reliable sources. You'll have contact information to get back to them, verify a fact, see if there's something that doesn't make sense and ask further questions, and all you do is include a list of thanks to everybody that helped you put the product together at the end of the book.

Email Options

You can create a similar project just using email, as my colleague Don Bice has done. It can happen amazingly quickly, just like a product originating from a newsgroup post, and it's very interesting to see how divergent the end product can be. **Just using email can send you in an entirely different direction than if you use newsgroups, even if your goal is the same**. In Don's case, he had certain newsletters that had a type of article in them that always did very well: articles with titles that start with something similar to "Ten Mistakes That People Make Doing…". For example, "Ten Mistakes Beginners Make in the Mail Order Business," and "Ten Mistakes Exhibitors Make at Trade Shows," are always very requested titles, since we're all fearful of making mistakes.

So Don took that as a direction: mistakes he could help people avoid, on subjects he could research by email and over the Internet that didn't require much writing. **The first step with something like this is to look for interesting or popular websites.** Now, this may take a little time. Maybe you'll find a list of the top fifty websites in your particular field -- or maybe you'll want to find a hundred websites that are popular in general. Let's say, for example, you want to offer a general interest product for people who want to have a more profitable or more successful website, while avoiding the pitfalls others have made along the way. What you want to do is find experts to write

---

this for you.

The first step is to compile a list of such sites. Then go to each of the websites and pull the email address of the person responsible for the site, assuming it's an individual; if it's a corporation, skip it and go to someone else because you want an individual to respond. **We're not talking about sites like Yahoo; we're talking about successful sites that are selling something, information or a product, or that have gotten a lot of media attention or a lot of traffic**. By some standard of your own, these, to you, are very successful sites. You may find them under any given search; the top sites that appear in any search engine are sure to get a lot of traffic. Identify the sites, as few or many as you want to take the time to collect.

Get the email addresses and write the owners an email letter; it can be a form letter, but not spam. Each letter should be addressed to the individual in charge of the site and it should mention their website.

That email letter should stroke their ego. Tell them you're writing a manual and contacting the individuals responsible for what you consider to be the most successful, innovative, profitable, high-traffic sites in your field. Ask for their help and tell them you'd like for them to contribute to your manual. What you're offering in return is to be in the manual: you'll publicize their website. You'll tell people how to go there to see what wonderful work they've done. Tell them you'd like for them to answer three questions for you: just three simple questions. It won't take much time. **By submitting their answers, they'll automatically give you the right to include them in your manual.**

Essentially, you're going to ask them things like, "What do you know now that you wish you'd known when you started? What do you think that you did, innovated, installed, or tried that contributed the greatest success to your site? What advice would you give to a company planning their first Internet site? What recommendation would you make that you think is key to their success?"

Ask them to reply at their earliest convenience. It's a simple thing for them to do. Some will, some won't -- but you just need to send out enough requests to get some material back.

When you get those responses back, you should have some interesting material with very revealing answers because some of these people will be quite articulate in their explanation of their success and especially articulate about any discoveries that they've made.

At this point, your job simply becomes one of sorting this information into logical groupings. You may want to group some of your information in a chapter titled, "*What I Wish I'd Known That I Didn't When I Started out.*"

You'll find that logical categories will present themselves. You don't have to write much -- you just cut, snip, and paste those emails. Put them into an electronic document, write an introduction, and you're done! You now have a product that you can give a title something like, "*The Secrets of a Successful Website, By 50 of the Most Successful Website Owners on the Internet.*" They'll tell people what they wish they'd known when they got started and you can make that a profitable experience.

Notice that I didn't say that you should ask them what mistakes they made. I think that's important. That was implied in any case, so you get a revelation of mistakes without calling it that. It still has a lot of the same appeal. Once you have all that information, you can pull it together into a product in much less than a day. Sure, you're going to have to spend a little pre-preparation time in getting the questionnaire together and

---

waiting for them to respond, but the actual assemblage of the product will take you less than a day. Then, you can either print it or offer it for sale on the Web. This is a natural product for electronic delivery, incidentally; your audience is already interested in, and on, the Web. Of course, you'll send a copy to each of the people who contributed, with your appreciation.

And there you are! In less than a day, you have a product that could be quite useful to your customer and quite profitable to you. **Now, remember: the fact you created the product quickly has absolutely no relationship to its value**. The number of pages or the number of hours you spent on it has no relationship to the value to your customers. What creates value for your customers is really very simple: what questions do they have that they really need to have answers to in order to succeed at whatever they're trying to accomplish? <u>If you ask good questions and provide good answers, you've built strong value into your product, no matter how quickly you created it</u>. When you start writing your ad copy, you want that value to remain in your head, so you can sell it. You want to be convinced of the value. So, don't short-change your work by saying, "I did it really quickly, so it couldn't be worth much." No -- if you did it quickly, you're just smart. It can still be worth a small fortune to the buyer.

Tap the Experts

Which brings us back to the fact that you don't necessarily have to be an expert in a field yourself in order to put together a successful product covering any subject. My colleague Jeff Gardner tells a story about helping a client who was in some pretty serious trouble. He called Jeff up and said, "Hey, look. I started my mail order business, but I'm kind of in a bind." Jeff said, "Well, explain it to me." The client said, "Well, I've got a fax machine, phone lines, computers, and I made contacts with printers, a mailing house, and all this stuff. I even bought my first ad in a magazine."

Jeff said, "Well, it sounds like you're off to a great start. What's the problem?"

The client said, "Um, I don't have a product." That's a big problem, especially after you've paid a couple hundred bucks for advertising in a magazine and the deadline's quickly coming up.

So Jeff asked him, "What do you want the product to be? Do you have any ideas?"

The client said, "I'd love it to be a product about making money in marketing. For example, it could be about all the different ways you can market products. It seems like that's a hot market. People would love to read that type of information in the place where I'm advertising. That's the kind of product I want to sell." Jeff said, "Okay, how much experience do you have? Could you write a product like that?"

The client said, said, "Uh, well, I've been doing this now maybe a month. I read all the books." So Jeff told him, "Okay, not too many people are going to buy a marketing book from a person who's had one month of experience and who's basically made no money in marketing. What you need to do is use this idea."

What Jeff told him to do was to tap some experts in the field -- and there are a lot of them. This is generally the case for any field, whether you're talking about making money or about horses or arts and crafts. In many cases, all you have to do is contact these experts and say, "Look, I'm compiling a product right now." Describe it and say something like, "I'd like to reprint your article, exactly the way it is in my own book. I won't edit it. I won't change a word. In exchange for that, I'll let you put any offer you want at the end of the article I put in the book." In many cases, that's the exact deal that these authors get with the magazines they publish in anyway: **their payment is free advertising at the end of the article.**

This client of Jeff's took his advice to heart because he contacted a lot of authors and experts, including my mentor and friend, Russ von Hoelscher, literally in one day. Many of them agreed and said, "Hey, take not only this article, but we've also got five, six, or seven others on marketing. Please print those in your book. Just make sure that at the end of each one, you give a little bit of context about us, our products, and how people can buy them. That's great. We'd love you to do that."

Within a day, then, Jeff's client had a compiled book on marketing, all from experts who'd been in the industry for a decade or more. It was almost immediately ready to sell, using the advertising he'd previously purchased. Of course, as print publications, it took him a little while to get all those articles. Then he had to go back and retype the information, reformat it, and put it into book format. **But basically, the authorization and all the articles were acquired within a one-day period.**

There's actually a way, using the Internet, where you can cut the process down and have the printed product of one or two hundred pages finished all within a single day. It's going to take some work, but it can be done. **This is how you do it.** A lot of these marketers and experts have their own websites. They put content on their websites. Many of these are free reports or excerpts from their books. They include many of those on their sites to get people interested in their other products. You can go to their websites and ask them the very same thing you would for a print publication: "Look, I'm putting this product together. I'd love to include your report. I'll give you a free plug at the end of that article if I can use it." In many cases, they'll say, "Yes!" Again, it's free advertising.

For example, Jeff Gardner once published an entire course on free advertising, which is one of his specialties. As he was updating it, he decided he wanted to put some additional information in there and really beef it up. At the same time, though, he didn't want to be stuck at the computer for the next six months, working his fingers to the bone. So he went to the Internet and found Paul Hartunion, a big name when it comes to free publicity. Jeff found that he had dozens of reports on the Internet, free for anybody to look at. Jeff quickly emailed him a request and he said, "Great. Please use these articles in your product. All I ask is free mention at the end."

So, instantly, Jeff had quite a bit of new information to add to his product -- probably an additional fifty or sixty pages that he was able to acquire instantly. **The best thing about this is that you can actually copy it right from the Internet and paste it into a document without having to retype a single word.** It's super simple. You can take this idea and use it for almost any niche, or any different idea, and there's your instant product.

Here's another great example, one that was literally a million-dollar product for us. Back in the early 1990s, Russ von Hoelscher used to travel to Kansas twice a year to consult with Eileen and I. I'll never forget the first time we picked him up in this old, dilapidated car and took him to this old, dilapidated farmhouse we lived in. Russ loved the place and it was a good deal -- we only paid a few hundred dollars a month for it -- but we wanted to get the heck out of there.

One of the ways we accomplished that was by means of a product we concocted after Russ went back and forth to Kansas for several years and consulted with us. Eileen came up with a great idea: she said, "Russ, instead of coming to Kansas and helping us with our marketing on an individual basis, let's create a product. Let's do some cassette tapes. We'll take one day where we'll ask you a lot of questions. You'll give us the answers, and we'll also put our input into it." It was just a super idea! We created a product called "*The $2,500 Weekend*" because that's what we were paying Russ. He'd fly in on Friday night and out on Sunday afternoon; in between that, mostly on Saturday, we'd work all day -- eight, nine, ten hours, or whatever -- on marketing. So right at our dining room table, we created "The $2,500 Weekend" tape in one long day and we had a lot of fun with it. A few years back we updated the product and changed the name from "*The $2,500 Weekend*" to "*The Millionaire Matrix.*" It continued to sell. **Both products sold for $195 and, together, we've sold millions of dollars worth.**

You can go to someone and collect your data or you can connect with them on a conference call by means of a conference call center that'll record the results. Or you can make do with some relatively cheap recording equipment that you can get from Radio Shack, although the conference center might be a little bit better, as far as quality goes (but not much). Get in touch with some people who are considered to be experts in their field and tell them you want to create a product by asking them all kinds of questions about what they do -- whether they're antique dealers, great marketers, chefs, or health experts. **Tell that that instead of paying them for this expertise, you'll give them rights to sell the final product**. Many of these experts will be happy to take that deal, especially if you massage their egos. You tell them how great they are. You tell them that you came to them because you think that they're the foremost experts in the field.

Using the example of Russ von Hoelscher again, a while back he got a call from Australia. The guy said he'd been working with Peter Sawn, Bill Myers, and others, putting together this package of expert information on mail order, the Internet, marketing, and the like. He went on to say, "I just have to have something from Russ von Hoelscher. I want to record you." He kept telling Russ how he thought he was great. Of course, our egos just start to melt under that kind of pressure. So Russ said, "Sure, when do you want to do it?" In the end, Russ gave him several hours of his time on a recording. You want to do the same thing the man who called Russ did with your experts because this is the way to get a product in one day with someone else doing most of the work. You can make a ton of money and it's a very, very exciting way to do it.

Don't Limit Your Options

In the previous scenarios, I've mostly been talking about audio recordings. Now, there are plenty of audio formats you can use and, of course, your options are increasing as technology evolves. You've got audiocassettes and audio CDs, but you can also provide MP3 files that people can play on their iPods. **Not only that, you could print the transcripts and create manuals as well. That gives you the opportunity to create multiple products from those same interviews**. If you happen to interview four or five people, you could make five audiotapes, five CD-ROMs, five MP3 sets, and five manuals. There are plenty of directions to take it in.

Using CD-ROM technology to create CD-ROMs is an especially effective direction to take this because, if you do it right, you can easily create a hot-selling product in a day or less. Let's say I decide to create a CD-ROM that's related to the Internet because the Internet is a hot topic right now, just as it has been for the past decade or so. **It's getting a lot of people excited. It's making a lot of people money.** Well, if you want to tap into that, you can spend a lot of time and energy writing and developing brand new Internet-related info -- or you can take advantage of what's already out there.

Go find websites where people are either giving away or

selling good reports. Contact them. Tell them that you're putting together a CD that's going to be a hot seller, and you know you've got a real winner here. Make them believe you can create a lot of exposure for them. Tell them that you'd like to list their report, or their manual if it's a small one, on your CD-ROM. In exchange, you'll provide a link so that people who read the report can go straight to their website.

By doing this, you can get as many items as a CD-ROM will hold -- dozens or even hundreds. This allows you to create a valuable product that you can sell profitably. But you can go even further than that and I recommend you do. For example, add a large link library of sites, all related to the topic of your CD. You can even sell advertising on the CD. **There are many, many things you can do to create a CD-ROM with a vast amount of value to your customer, all in a day**. It's easy to get this information; again, just go to people and massage their egos, tell them how great their websites are, that you love them, and ask them if you can include their report on your CD. You'd like to give them free mention and you'll be sure to include a link to their website. A lot of them, you'll find, will be happy to do that for you.

There are at least three different ways to use this CD-ROM to make money.

First of all, you can simply sell it yourself. You can slap a price tag on it, virtually any price, because CD-ROMs are absurdly cheap to duplicate. If you find the right supplier, you can get them done in quantity for as little as fifty cents. But you could sell your CD for as anywhere from $19.95, if it doesn't have a lot of information on it, to as much as $99, $150, or $200 if it's information-dense.

Another way you can sell it is to create a distributorship and let your customers sell it for you. In our business, people like to sell products. If you have a customer base, you could set up a distributorship and let them buy the CDs from you in small quantities for a few dollars apiece, so you'll make a profit on each CD-ROM that way. Then, they can go ahead and sell them and they can keep a nice profit on each one they sell.

Finally, you can sell master rights. Maybe you've got other people who are interested in your CD; it's taking off like wildfire and you're getting a lot of sales. Some people who would actually pay you $500, $1,000, $2,000, or even as much as $5,000 for the rights to duplicate your CD-ROM, just like you do. In addition to selling your CD, you can also give it away as a premium to people who buy another one of your products; after all, it cost just fifty cents to make.

So there are lots of things you can do with a CD-ROM, especially if it has something to do with the Internet or covers a hot topic that you know people are interested in. Some people ask, "How do you make these huge products?" **Well, they're often just collections of existing products.**

If You Can Talk, You Can Write

Another way to put together a quick information product is to record yourself or another expert in the process of teaching people how to do a specific task.

I'm going to use my colleague Mark Nolan as an example of how this can work. Mark once had a small advertising agency where he'd teach people how to get free publicity through news releases and the like since running paid ads in most publications is beyond the means of many companies, especially the little start-ups. He started talking about this at chambers of commerce and similar places and, eventually, he was invited to teach an adult education class at a couple of the community colleges close by.

Every community college has these classes -- everything from "How to Cook Italian Food," to "How to Flirt," to "How to Fix Your Car." Mark's was on how to get free publicity for your business. It was just a three-hour class. They're normally for a relatively small set price, and the instructor gets about half of that. This one, I think, was $48, and Mark would have 50 or so people show up. For three hours of work, he'd make hundreds of dollars.

One day a young lady asked him, "Can I record this so I can listen to it over and over? Then, I'll have the handout materials and I'll be able to study them while I listen to the tape." **Mark said, "You know, I should have thought of that.** That's a brilliant idea! I'd be happy to have you tape it if I can have a copy of it and use it for whatever I want." She said, "Of course!" She had a very good tape recorder and she sat right in the front as she recorded it. Several days after the class, she gave Mark a good, clean copy of the talk he'd been giving. Next, he had it transcribed and, when he added the handout material, my goodness, he had a book! He was an author!

So Mark edited it, started selling it, and it became extremely popular. In his own advertising, he'd say, "Are you trying to grow your business? Here's how to get millions of dollars in free advertising. I give this talk. I get paid hundreds of dollars to teach this, but in this format, it's only $29.95." He ended up selling 100,000 copies of it, making about $3 million in sales -- and it all started with a talk.

Before trying this yourself, I'd recommend getting a copy of the book *You Can Write If You Can Think*.

The authors tell you that if you can talk, then you can

write. It's all a matter of capturing your words somehow -- and these days, there are technological tricks that make that easy. They even have voice recognition software that you load onto your computer so you can talk directly to your computer, which then transcribes what you say. If you say, "It was a dark and stormy night," the words appear on the computer screen. It's almost spooky.

You can also videotape a course and make a book out of that. If you want a higher-priced product, just put the audio and the video together with the printed book; then you have a package. <u>If you don't have something that you want to speak on, or you're just not comfortable giving a talk, you can always make a deal with another expert to sell their products</u>. This may be anything that you're interested in and don't consider yourself an expert at. I'm not an expert on NASCAR, but if I went to Jeff Gordon and interviewed him the way we've been talking about, that would be a legitimate product. Instead of pretending that I knew everything about NASCAR, I'd go to an expert.

The way you can do that with these community college courses is to start by getting their Adult Education catalog. Look through it and see what classes interest you. Mark Nolan lives in wine country and loves to go wine tasting, though he doesn't consider himself an expert by any means. But he knows a guy who really is quite a wine expert, who teaches a class on it at a nearby college; he tells you all about why wines taste a certain way, why one tastes so good and another doesn't, and he also tells you about all the different wine regions, so there's a travelogue aspect involved, too.

One day Mark asked him, "May I videotape you?" and he said, "I'd be delighted!" Mark told him that he would give him a master copy and that he could do anything he wanted to with it, if Mark could keep one and sell it if he wanted.

All the expert wanted was for Mark to put his name and address at the end so that people could write to him and he could sign them up for his class or sell them his newsletter. <u>So, instead of pretending he was a wine expert, Mark interviewed this guy -- and then he had a video he could sell</u>. At the time Mark had a wine tasting website, so that tape was a good product to sell on the site.

All this comes out of those little adult education classes at your local community college. **You can create an audio recording; you can make a video; you can make it into a book. Basically you end up with an instant product within a day or two, at least once you find someone that's happy to do it -- and most of them are.**

Practice Makes Perfect

As I wrap up this chapter, I want to point out one important thing about informational products. At M.O.R.E. Inc. we've produced hundreds of them over the past few decades -- and they just keep getting easier. **That's something you should keep in mind as you advance in your career: the more you do, the easier it gets, until all of this becomes very simple.**

Here's another point I'd like to re-emphasize, and it's not going to be the last time you hear it, either. **As long as you're providing good information to your specific market, who cares if it just took you a day or less to produce?** As I mentioned earlier, we produced that "*$2,500 Weekend*" program with Russ von Hoelscher in a day. Now, when we first found out about this business, we bought a book called *Twenty-Five Thousand Dollars For A Few Hours' Work Doesn't Seem Fair*. But even though we fell in love with the idea of self-publishing, we always thought, "We'll never make $25,000 working a few hours." Wrong!

When you average out the time we spent on that one product with Russ, we made over $50,000 an hour. That's taking the profits from that book, not gross sales. So it's possible; <u>I can prove it from my own results</u>.

Again, you're getting paid for the product sold. It doesn't have anything to do with the amount of time that you spend on it.

Since then, we've produced many products the same way. The first product we ever did with Alan R. Bechtold was when he came to our studio and we recorded a product -- in a single day -- called "*The $3,000 a Day Marketing Expert*" because that's what Alan charged. It was the same concept we used with Russ, though we turned it into something a little bit different.

You can do many different products by using new slants and coming up with ideas that are similar. Many times we've gone down to the studio and recorded round-table conversations that just took a few hours -- and then proceeded to sell many thousands of copies of that product. I want to make this point very clear: **it's the value in the product you're creating that matters, not how much it costs you to produce it**.

CHAPTER THREE

"Formulas for Profit"

It always pays not to have to reinvent the wheel and, in this chapter, I'll show you how to generate content for your quick products without having to create it from scratch every single time. **There are many ways you can do this, from tapping experts for free (something I covered in detail in the last chapter) to purchasing or licensing other content**. You can even develop and use an existing boilerplate that can be quickly and easily modified for your new products.

Ever-Changing Web Content

Many of us are attracted by the concept of information products that we can sell electronically, particularly on a website. That said, you can also create valuable products to give away, simply in order to attract users who will then buy your other products and services. The problem, of course, is coming up with the necessary content. **The trick is to put it together as quickly as possible and still make it valuable.**

One of the neatest (if most challenging) ways to offer a product is to provide content that changes frequently so people will bookmark your site and return frequently to see what's new.

It's not as tough as you might think. **A simple, effective way to do this is to go to a site that offers syndicated content from columns to blogs to RSS feeds.** One of the first companies that did this was Isyndicate.com; it's since become YellowBrix (www.yellowbrix.com) and it's still offering the same kind of content (among other things). You just sign up to get your own user ID and password and go from there. They provide top news along with info on weather, sports, business and finance, opinions and advice columns, earth sciences, health, fun and games, lifestyles and entertainment, and other information and articles that you can use on your website. These are provided by the likes of Reuters, AP, and UPI; all of the biggest companies. This used to be free, but now they charge for it. A free source that's similar is Freesticky (http://www.freesticky.com), which provides games, news, articles, weather, and even comics.

The bottom line is that they give you a little snip of the code; once you sign up you can plant this into your website code and after that, the items are updated and changed and modified for you. Then every time you go to the site, there's new news popping up there. **What you've just created is an information product you can literally display on the Web to attract users who come back and visit more and more often**. If Freesticky and YellowBrix don't work for you, don't worry -- there are other services you can try. All it takes is a little research on Google to find them.

Perennial Content

While it's great to have constantly renewing content, perennials always work well -- that is, products that sell well year in and year out. Business start-up manuals (for any kind of business in the world) are good examples. I can't think of anyone who, at some point in their life, hasn't dreamed of going into business for themselves.

One of the first things they do once they make that decision is to purchase information that tells them how to start that business they're dreaming about. There's a way those types of manuals can be created very easily, especially if you already have CD-ROMs, print reports, and so forth that contain a lot of business start-up information. **You can create a start-up information on just about any subject by building a boilerplate template and simply filling in the blanks.**

For example, "*How to make Money in (blank)*" -- and then you put in the name of a business and you're off and running. **You can start with the public domain information you can gather off the Internet. That will give you a 5-15 page report that offers the basics of a start-up**. Then you find someone who's in that business and ask them if you can interview them about their experience, their advice, how they feel about the business, the pitfalls that they've had to watch out for, and the opportunities that they see for other people entering that business. You can easily do a recorded telephone interview with that person or even an email interview.

For instance, if you decide to do a start-up manual on "*How to Form a Desktop Publishing Business*" you'd find someone local who has a desktop publishing business and you would approach them and ask them if they would be kind enough to do an interview and share their success story. **You'd think that most people wouldn't, that they wouldn't want to create more competition -- but you generally encounter just the opposite.** These folks are so flattered that you'd ask for their opinion that they're more than happy to help you.

Telephone interviews are the best kind for several reasons: they're less stressful for people, they fit into their schedules more easily, and they're much easier for most people than going into a recording session. You just make a list of questions you'd like to ask them, send them the list in advance so they have no surprises and they're comfortable, and then call them up at the appointed time. Chat a few minutes, then start your recording, and do an interview for an hour or less.

So now you have the report and you have an audiotape.

If you want to add more value you can transcribe that tape and add it to your package -- and now you add the frosting.

Frosting is information on how you start your own business, how you do the bookkeeping, how you do advertising, how you do marketing. **All that information is available free from the Small Business Administration**. You can write them for the material or you can go to their website at http://www.sba.gov. Not only can you download basic information, but there's even some software you can download that's all public domain -- which means it's free for you to copy and distribute. Now, you can put all this together in a package you can sell from anywhere from $45 to $100 that represents real value for the buyer because it gets them started in the right direction.

So there you are: you've established a formula. **You can go down a list of popular businesses that people have an interest in starting, then quickly create a whole series of these reports that will sell year in and year out**. The old ones are selling even while you're creating new ones. If you're really lazy, like some of us are, you may find that once you've established this format, you can have a college student come in and duplicate these for you. They can take your format and ask the same questions of other businesspeople and, suddenly, you've got a whole series going with little or no effort.

The Right Direction

Directories have always been very popular -- so much so that there's a directory of directories. Go to any large library in your area and take a look; you'll discover that directories are hot sellers. There are a lot of them out there, covering a variety of topics. For example, there are directories of bed and breakfasts all across the U.S., arts and crafts shows, vacation spots that welcome pets, or discounts for seniors. All are just compilations of sources that offer a particular thing to a particular group of people.

The best thing about this type of product is that you're not doing much creative writing. Basically, all you're doing is pulling together a variety of sources that a niche market would be interested in. It can be very simple to do and it's particularly powerful when you tie it together with the Internet. If you want to create a directory very quickly, then the Internet is going to be your number one tool for doing so; you may even be able to create your directory in less than a day, since it's easy to find data if you know what you're looking for.

Let's say, for example, you're creating a directory on freebies. Let's be more specific: free things for children. Well, you can get on any of the major search engines and look for companies that offer freebies for children. Within a couple of hours you can have a big list of such companies. You can compile that list into a print product that you can immediately start selling. **And because the Internet is always growing, you're always going to have new sources of information for your directories.**

The good thing about a directory (at least from your perspective!) is that not only can you sell it long-term, but the information in the directory will, over time, become outdated. The directory that someone buys today will be completely outdated within two or three years. **They're going to want to come back to you again and again to purchase updated directories.** So, you might have a customer who purchases an initial directory from you; then, maybe next year when you have your newest edition out and the year after that when you have another new edition, they come back to purchase those versions. **This can become an excellent profit center for your business.**

You can even offer access to a website, as a bonus for people who purchase your directory, and keep updated information there. Let's say someone purchases the print directory. You're only able to update that at best every six months, but probably you'd rather update it every year or two. With a website, you can update it every hour or every minute, if you want. You can tell your customers, "Purchase the directory now and you'll get a secret password to our website where we keep all our updated, new sources that we constantly research on a day-by-day basis." That can be a very valuable bonus.

Plus, as you're updating the directory on your website, you can take that information directly and plug it into your new, updated print edition every year. Then, instead of trying to do it all at once, you're doing it over time. It makes the job of creating a directory very simple and very fast. And if you're careful, you can get someone else to pay for the printing. For example, Russ von Hoelscher has a friend named Al Galasso who's been publishing a drop-ship book dealer's directory for about nine years. **Every year, not only does he update the directory and sell thousands of copies of it, but he also puts paid advertising in the back of his directory.** He likes to brag, sometimes, that the advertisers pay for the printing.

Profiting from Someone Else's Work (While They Profit Too!)

Believe it or not, there's a way to become an instant publisher while letting other people do all the work. They can write the book, they can typeset the book, they can even publish the book -- then you get the book to sell and make money with.

Every year, there are about 60,000 or 70,000 books published in America alone. Only about 100 of them become bestsellers, though there are a few thousand others that sell well and make both the authors and publishers money. But the majority of books published in America today -- as much as 90%, or even more -- either just break even or lose money. The big publishers in New York are to blame because they put out hundreds of books a year and seriously market only a few of them. They expect only a small percentage to sell, so they put the big budgets behind their top authors. **They'll spend hundreds of thousands or millions of dollars on promotion, sure, but just for the big guys.**

If you're Tom Clancy, John Grisham, or Michael Creighton, they're going to give you a million-dollar push. If you're an unknown or new author, you're going to get very little or no promotion money. **So, what happens is that most of these books die on the vine very quickly.** The bookstores make the matter even worse because they take in a few copies of each book from the publishers and toss them up on the shelf. If they have no promotion, they die there. After a month and a half or so, they just take them down and send them right back to the publishers.

Whether you're looking for a cookbook, a health book, a business book, or an investment book, you can go to one of these bookstores and peruse the bargain book tables. **If you see a book that was $29.95 a few months or a year ago and now it's marked $4.95 or $5.95, discounted 80% or more, you know this is a book that the publishers have given up on.** Now, you have to be careful, of course -- sometimes you have bestsellers that sold hundreds of thousands of copies, and maybe they printed 25,000 or 50,000 too many the last time, or maybe they're going to switch it paperback in just a few months, so they might take that last 25,000 or 50,000 copies and dump them on the remainder book market. Those are books they're not going to make deals on with you because they're expecting all kinds of future sales and different editions.

You're looking for authors who are lesser known, but who've written good books in your field of interest. Find out who the publisher is, then go directly to them and offer to buy the rights; it may cost as little as $500 to get them. Tell these publishers, "I'm not looking for the bookstore rights. I'll sign a document that states that I won't put these books in the bookstores; I'm looking to sell them by mail." Or tell them, "I want to sell them on the Internet only." When you get the rights, it's a good idea to offer 100 copies or so at a big discount to first see if your idea is good, that this book will be a good seller. Once you've done that, you can publish that book yourself, printing 1,000, 2,000, or more copies, and all the publisher will require is that you pay a royalty. It could be a dollar, a dollar and a half, or two dollars that the publisher and the author will share.

Why will the publishers give you the rights to some of their books cheaply? Simply because 80-90% of their books aren't selling. They're on the remainder market already. They've given up on them. They're dying a slow death and the publishers are happy to have someone come along and say, "I just want the Internet and direct mail rights to this book." This is an outstanding way to get a ready-made book cheaply that you can then test, especially if you can get some copies from the publisher. If it's a good seller, then go ahead and publish it yourself. Even if you had to pay $1,000 or $2,000 for the rights, remember: you didn't have to write the book. You didn't have the book typeset. You're not the original publisher. A lot of things have been done for you already that take a lot of money, time, and effort.

This is a great way to find books that haven't made it in the marketplace despite the fact that they're good books. Generally, they just haven't been promoted correctly. As a direct marketer and someone who's learning how to sell on the Internet, you can grab these treasures and make some serious money with them. **In fact, once you own the rights to one of those books,**

you can slap it up on Amazon.com and let them help sell it for you. You can instantly become a publisher who has a book that's being sold on a major Internet site.

A Book of Lists

Another option is to publish a book or manual that lists proven website sales letters and promotions. Again, you don't have to do much writing and you can easily put the product together in a day or less.

If you go to any site that sells something, there's going to be a sales letter there and probably some promotional materials, too. **What you want to do is look for websites that look good, but also sell products and are making the people who own the websites a lot of money.** If you visit Internet newsgroups, you'll discover that a lot of people are interested in how other people are making money on the Internet. It doesn't matter, really, what the subject area is; you could choose to focus on one specific market or you can cover all kinds of websites.

It would probably be better if you focused on one specific niche market, however, because then you could show people in that market other websites like theirs that are making money.

Find out who people are talking about on the newsgroups; if someone has asked a question about how a website is successful, see who's responded that their website is doing ten thousand dollars a month in sales. **Once you find those successful individuals, go to them and tell them you're publishing a new book and you'd like to use them as an example**. Many times you'll find that they'll be happy to let you do that. Ask them for permission to reprint their sales letter in your book and compile a list. If the average letter is five pages and you had ten of them in your book, you'd have fifty pages. If you had 100 proven websites, you'd have 500 pages. You could have two, three, or four volumes of proven Internet promotions and sales letters that you could sell. **You could sell them on the Internet in digital format, as "e-books," and you can deliver them right over the Internet via email.** On the other hand, you can also create print versions; there are lots of things you could do with your compilation.

I know, firsthand, that there are a lot of people out there who are interested in seeing what's working on the Internet, so a book on this subject would do extremely well.

Easy, Ingenious Ideas

Sometimes an idea is so unique, so revolutionary, that it can practically create itself in a day or two. For example: a friend was in an airport gift shop a few years back, killing some time while he was waiting for his flight and he saw this book sitting right on the counter by the cash register: *Everything Men Know About Women*. So, of course, he picked it up, since like most men he knew almost nothing about women. He opened it, and all the pages were blank -- so, obviously, here's somebody with a good sense of humor who created this book in less than one day. All they had to do was come up with a nice cover; the rest was blank, every single page. He asked the clerk, "Does this sell well?" and she said, "It's a bestselling book and it's not even a book!" She was flabbergasted. But you know, people need to laugh. That's why comedians are some of the highest paid people in the entertainment industry.

Another instant product that my friend Mark Nolan helped a lot of people with when he was a list broker consisted, simply, of all their customer names. They'd come up to him and say, "Gosh, we're having a cash flow problem," or "We're trying to grow our business and what we want to do is to move into a building and acquire some equipment. So what we need to do is increase our sales?" Mark would always find this hidden asset they had, since he knew about lists and they didn't. He'd ask, "How many customer names are in your computer?" and they might say, "We've got seventeen thousand names." Well, dump those on a disk and there's your product. Take it to a list manager and they'll start renting it for you -- the next thing you know, you'll be getting a big check. Wouldn't you like for a $10,000 check to show up in the mail for doing nothing? **Your customer lists are great instant products, if you've been in business a while.**

Here's another idea: republish something in the public domain. Here's a book that's already been written some years ago and has stood the test of time -- but it's fallen out of copyright. This applies to more than books, by the way. For[7] example, the movie It's a Wonderful Life, with Jimmy Stewart, is in the public domain, which means that you can copy it and sell it if you like. But be very, very careful when making assumptions about whether something's in the public domain or not; copyrights can be renewed. <u>If you find something you think is out of copyright but you're unsure, contact the U.S. Copyright Office for a ruling</u>. You send them a fee and they'll tell you whether or not the item is out of copyright. When you have that letter, you're obviously protected legally.

Two books that I know are in the public domain are "Scientific Advertising" by Claude Hopkins, which is a classic that most marketers worth their salt have read a half-dozen times, and "As a Man Thinketh" by James Allen, another wonderful classic; it was written over a hundred years ago, but it's still in print. Well, Mark Nolan once needed some bonus gifts to give away to his customers. He didn't have time to create them so reprinted both books. He edited "As a Man Thinketh" slightly because there are some terms in there that have gone out of common usage.

For example, Allen talks about how to rise above beggary; today we call it poverty, so Mark changed that one word. Mostly, though, he stayed very true to the original; he just wrote a short introduction, added it to the beginning, and retitled it to *As You Think So Shall You Become*, simply because he wanted to make it clear that it applied to women as well as men. It took a morning to put that together and have it printed and, suddenly, Mark had a book that he's since given away thousands of copies of. He's even sold copies of it: you can go into any bookstore and ask for that book and they'll order it for you, straight from Mark. You can also order it from Amazon.com. Mark reprinted "Scientific Advertising" in much the same way, for much the same reasons.

Now, you might say, "Well, I already have a product." **But imagine if you use these methods I've already talked about where you audiotape a lecture or a telephone seminar or interview someone on the phone**. You throw that product in. Then, you get this "As You Think" book and you toss that in. Pretty soon you begin to have a real course, not just a small information product. **Everybody needs a free bonus gift and those books have worked well for Mark**.

There are all kinds of other books that are available. **A good product might be to collect a lot of these and put them all on a CD-ROM**. Then, you could sell this to people and say, "Here are 25 products you can have the rights to." A lot of people would buy that. <u>The government, for example, has a ton of material that's in the public domain; your tax dollars paid for it</u>. You can order the Consumer Information catalog from the Consumer Department of Information in Pueblo, Colorado; it's filled with books, reports, booklets, and the like. To use Mark Nolan as an example again, he once pulled together different items called "How To Teach Your Child To Read," "How To Teach Your Child Math," "How To Use The Library," and "How To Increase Spelling Proficiency and Win Spelling Tests," and put those all together with a little coloring book he was selling that taught phonics to preschoolers, with a tagline that said, "Reprinted from the government publication." **People loved it: they got more than they thought they would get. It really made that a better package.**

I love the idea of using CD-ROMs to their full potential. At M.O.R.E. Inc. we have a CD-ROM that has something like 4,164 pages of text on it. Just to see how much that was, we printed all of those pages out on paper -- and it came to 45 pounds of material! It's incredible, the amount of information you can put on one CD-ROM.

Clear Out the Cobwebs of Confusion

This is an exciting time to be alive because you have so many options when it comes to creating products quickly -- but I don't want to pretend that it's easy. **It takes a lot of work and a substantial understanding of the options**.

While some of this book's readers are poring over these ideas I've presented and thinking, "Well, that sounds pretty good," I expect some of you are still a little bit confused about how to begin and what product to start with. That's nothing to be embarrassed about -- honestly, I think there are a lot of people out there who are confused about these subjects. My wife Eileen and I certainly were.

The way to get started is simply to get started. Okay, so maybe you won't get it right the first time; Eileen and I didn't. I remember the very first time we ever sat down to write a booklet. It was a failure; we never even finished it. But the second time we did finish our product. It was only sixteen pages long and it's embarrassing to look at now, but the people we sold it to loved it. We used that small booklet, which measured just five- and-a-half by eight-and-a-half inches, to launch our information empire.

If you're a little bit confused about all these ideas and you're wondering how in the world you can get started and which ideas are the right ones, here's something that can help you greatly. **While it may be a little difficult to get started, once you have your customer base -- a group of customers who have bought something from you, anything at all -- your concerns about what product to sell and who to sell it to are going to go away.** That's how it was with Eileen and me. Once we sold our first little sixteen-page booklet, it became very easy for us to figure out what to sell to that customer base. We knew that they liked our booklet; they wrote to us and told us and even talked to us on the telephone. And here's the second part of this equation: we knew a lot about these people because we were the kind of people who bought the kinds of products we were now selling. **You have to intimately know your customers to succeed in this business.**

Here's one of my best tips for you. **Find a market you love, come up with a great benefit-driven headline title, and break that subject down so it's easy to follow**: for example, "*Seven Steps to Get Rich With Your Website.*" Simply create an informational product using some of the ideas I've talked about here and market it. Once you do, you'll have a group of customers you have a relationship with. They'll buy from you again and again. The better you can get to know these people, the easier it's going to be for you.

So, the question doesn't become, "My God, what can I sell to these people?" All of a sudden, the question is, "I've got dozens of things I can sell to these people. What are the best products I can sell to them?" It's a different problem than sitting around scratching your head, trying to figure out what to sell. Ask yourself, "What can I sell that's going to do the very best?" **If you're confused right now, just keep this in mind: it does get easier!** It gets simpler, especially when you have a group of hungry customers who will continue to buy from you again and again. Russ von Hoelscher first taught us that principle back in 1988.

There's no question that the hardest part is starting without one person on your customer list. That's why I think it's so important to sell something cheap in the beginning -- or even to give something away free. But you can't give away junk: it must be something with perceived value that will allow you to build a potential customer list. **Russ always says that you start with inquiries and then you turn those inquiries into buyers.** Once they've bought something, move on to the next step: turn those buyers into customers who will buy repeatedly. Once you have a mailing list, then you have people you can bring your new offers to. That's crucial!

One of the biggest problems most people have when getting into the self-publishing business is cash flow -- they don't have a lot of it. If you're spending six months or a year trying to create your very first product, you have absolutely no cash flow that entire time. **That's why it's so very important to start by creating an instant product so you can get that cash flowing and build that customer base.** Later on, if you want to create a product that takes six months or a year, you can do that; but at the beginning, you need money coming in so you can build your business. Creating instant products, or products that take a couple days or a week, is very important because just getting started is the key.

There's never been a better time than now to build a customer list by giving something away. Thanks to the Internet, you don't have the expense involved in printing and mailing a free product in order to gather names and addresses. You can utilize the Internet as the delivery mechanism to send a valuable free product for next to nothing to thousands of people.

The information itself goes to them electronically, in return for their mailing information and email address, and that builds a list at essentially no cost to you, except of course for developing the product. **The secret is providing true value for your customers and helping them to get more of what they bought from you the first time.**

It's my experience that when you really feel an affinity with your customers, when you create informational products for them, you almost feel like you're doing it for a friend. I think there's a real power in creating an information product on something you have an interest in or for a group of people you want to help. It's not like you're trying to market to people you don't have anything in common with; you're marketing to someone who may be just like you. **You're creating a product that has a lot of value to you and is interesting to you.** People who are like you might have the exact same interest and may be willing to buy it. It creates an amazing level of camaraderie with your customers.

I think that's especially important in self-publishing endeavors because, if you create products that have a high value to you and you're selling to people who are just like you, you're going to gain a lot of respect and credibility with your customer base. Believe me, you'd rather have that type of respect and credibility when you're selling them product number two, three, or three hundred and three than just trying to slam them on some horrible ten page stapled-together report that has virtually no information in it. You're going to get a lot further if you feel a camaraderie, and have a win-win relationship with your customers, than if you're just trying to scam them and make that quick ten or twenty dollar sale.

Again, you're selling something that you love. You're building a relationship with people so they will come back and buy from you again and again and again. That's the secret to long-term wealth.

CHAPTER 4

"Selling and Reselling Yourself"

In an earlier chapter, I mentioned situations where you could plant the seed and then come back and harvest a wealth of information a few days or weeks later and use that information to create quick, hot-selling products. In some cases, however, you can do the harvesting in a day or less -- in fact, it can take you just a few minutes. I've already mentioned putting together product or service directories and similar products; they sell very well on the newsstands, in bookstores, and by mail. **Well, one of the greatest ways to get product information about what's new, what's hot, and what's being developed is through press releases.** The beauty of a press release is that when the company sends you a press release, it's material that's written and ready to go.

In the past, some of my colleagues and I have had excellent luck listing ourselves as authors, publishers, or editors with Bacon's Information Incorporated, which is now called Cision (http://us.cision.com/). Once you get yourself listed in their huge directories, which go out to P.R. firms all over the world, you'll start getting press releases that you can just gather together on the topics of your choice and then use them to create a directory with detailed info about new products.

Another great place is a company called E-Releases (http://www.ereleases.com). You can join immediately and start receiving the press releases they distribute to their customers by email. You'll also find all kinds of other interesting leads

---

and ways that they'll be happy to put together stories for you.

So now you're in touch with P.R. professionals. What are they going to do? They're going to write the stuff for you.

Reformulate, Reprofit

Here's another easy way to make more money on products you've already been selling: change the format. Let's say you have a CD-ROM you're selling that's got hundreds of reports designed to sell from $1-$5. They've sold for years in that form. But aha -- people like information nowadays in all sorts of forms. What if you just converted those simple reports, which you already own the rights to, into audiotapes or audio CDs?

That opens up a whole new market, because it creates a whole new product; there are people who'll purchase audiotapes who will never purchase printed reports. Besides, the audio files have a much higher perceived value, though they're usually cheaper to duplicate than the reports. People are used to paying $10-20 for tapes and audio CDs so they're happy to pay that.

What you do is find a subject heading that you can group a number of reports under, like *Making Money At Home, Making Money With Your Computer, Making Money In Mail Order*.

Look through the assortment of reports you have, or those that are out there on the market, and figure out a way to do a grouping of these tapes. Now, instead of selling one or two reports, you can record a report on each side of the tape. You can put together a set of four tapes or six tapes easily in a day, or create a single CD with all those things on it. **You now have a product that can sell for $40, $50, or $60, instead of the $1-$5 each for the reports.** You have a larger sale, a different product for a different market, and it's an easy product to put together.

If you don't like to record or feel you don't have a voice for recording, get a friend to record it or read the report thoroughly and have someone interview you about the information. It's a very easy way to put a product together. If some of your recordings are a little short on time, you can use some of the public domain material from the SBA office on starting a small business, bookkeeping, marketing, and so forth to fill them out, as I mentioned earlier.

Back-End Options

Here's a question I often get from people about creating these instant products:

"Okay, I can create an audio recording, manual, directory, or whatever within a day. Now I've got a $20 product, when I know that a lot of my back-end sales need to be $195, $295, or more. How in the heck am I going to do that?"

Well, why not take a number of these one-day ideas and put together a larger package? You can do it in a week or less by focusing on a product a day. Or let's say you're lazy; you want to create a brand new product every two days. (Remember, it's not months. It's not years.) Give yourself a week or two to polish it up and get everything ready and you can have a course that you might sell for $195, $295, or $495 or more, just from using a number of these ideas together. It still takes you a relatively short amount of time. Whereas, if you did some conventional creative writing, that same type of a course might take you two years or longer to create.

Take a Novel Approach

In a preceding chapter, I talked about how a friend encountered this book that you could create not just in one day, but in probably ten minutes: *Everything Men Know About Women*. Of course, all the pages in this book are blank except for the cover and front matter.

Well, Russ von Hoelscher has a similar story he likes to tell. He was speaking once at one of Robert Allen's seminars in San Diego and a woman came up to him during the break and showed him that book. She said, "Russ, have you got any good ideas on how I can sell more of these books?"

Being the marketing guru he is, Russ looked at the book and kind of smiled and said, with great wisdom, "You know, I've seen a few of these books over the years, but I just don't know if they sell or not."

She said, "Russ, I'm not asking you whether it's a good seller. I've already sold a million copies in the last two years! I was just asking you if you have any unusual or different ideas on how I can sell more copies."

Well, Russ just about fell over; over a million copies in just a couple years, of a book with blank pages!

Later, Russ was talking to Al Galasso about that and Al said, "Oh yeah, one of the authors we're promoting has a book that's doing well during the election. It's "All The Best Reasons Why You Should Re-Elect Bill Clinton." Of course, he sent Russ a copy of it, he opened it up, and found that all the pages were blank.

So put on your thinking cap. Try something novel. This kind of book is the easiest and cheapest book you'll ever create and one you could make a lot of money with if you come up with the right idea. People like this stuff. They've already done the thing about women and, of course, Clinton got re-elected anyhow.

What other ideas could you come up with? It has to be something that really tickles the funny bone. This could be a real moneymaker for you. **It's simple and, sure, it's a gimmick -- but it's a heck of a profit center.** There are so many ideas you could pursue; you could just sit down in an hour or so while you're watching TV in the evening and think of all the comical titles you could make for these blank books. You could have a fifty page book, a three hundred page book, it doesn't matter; the printing is cheap when you're printing blank pages!

Record Your Thoughts

At this point, I want to reiterate something I've already discussed. I think it's an important issue, and something that can really help people to at least get started, but I want to take it in a slightly different direction than I did before. Earlier, I told you about Mark Nolan's experience, with his community college class, where he had his lecture taped and ended up using that as the basis for a product that made him $3 million. You can do the same thing, easily. **There are a lot of people**

out there who have a lot of information stored in their heads about various topics and they could create a valuable information product if they would just record their thoughts.

The first time you do it, it doesn't have to be great quality. You could sit down with a plain-jane tape recorder, record your thoughts and get some practice at how to articulate yourself, and do it over and over again until you perfect it. Then you can record a product. I know of some people who've even produced tapes that you would think of as poor quality and still made money. People have done the same thing with videotapes, where the video itself has been poor quality but the information has been high quality. **So don't be too concerned about the quality when you first put your own ideas on tape**.

Take a topic, a subject, that you know a lot about and just sit down and record yourself for 30, 60, or 90 minutes, or as long as you can go on a topic. Then you've got yourself a hot product you've just created in less than a few hours. **You can take that tape and turn it into a transcript, so you can give away the written word along with the audiotape; you can put it in digital format and sell it on your website or you can let people download the written transcript.** There are many, many things you can do with audiotapes. If you don't want to record yourself, again, record other experts in the field that you're interested in. Get them to talk about it for you and sell them giving their advice. Just remember: audiotape, and audio on CD-ROM, is one of the easiest ways you can create fast products that you can sell for a lot of money.

Simplify Your Life

I think most people try to make things too complicated, so do what you can to keep your product simple. **For example, I like to tell people about a very simple, short little book that's sold one billion copies.** Not a million but a billion, with a B. People always think that if a book's sold a billion copies, it's got to be some incredible, amazingly ambitious and earthshaking book. I just say, "Of course it is. **The name of this book is *The Poky Little Puppy*."**

The *Poky Little Puppy* is a Little Golden Book, the kind you read to your five-year-old kid. And yes, it has sold a billion copies. So if you think you have to write *Gone With The Wind*, well, just remember that *Poky Little Puppy*. My friend Mark Nolan tells me he has a copy of that book in his office, sitting where he can see it. Every time he gets too involved in some major *Gone with the Wind* type of book project, he just looks at *The Poky Little Puppy* and bursts out laughing.

The last time he looked at it, he tells me, he was saying to himself, "I should come up with some new challenge, something interesting, that would be fun to do every month." His wife said, "Why don't you start a newsletter? Everybody's always asking us, 'Can I subscribe to Mark's newsletter?' I have to tell them 'What newsletter?' We don't have a newsletter." Well, being a self-described lazy guy, Mark decided he didn't want to have to write it every month. Then he realized that he gets so much information in the mail, off the Internet, and from people he networks with that he has enough to sell two newsletters every month. **What he does is take notes of what people say and prints out things off of the Internet. He tears things out of magazines and puts it all in a box.** At the end of the month, sure enough, Mark has more than enough material to put in a newsletter -- so he started one, in just a day.

He sat down and said, "Let me see if I can write a prototype issue #1."

So he did and it was great, so he printed it and sent it out. He was happy with it, and wanted to see if anyone else thought it was the slightest bit interesting, so he offered it as a yearly subscription -- and all of the sudden, the checks started pouring in.

You only need one issue to start an eight-page newsletter and you can type it on a computer, just like a letter. It doesn't have to be typeset. If you want it to be typeset, well, just use Microsoft Publisher or a similar program that offers a variety of templates. You just take the information you've typed, you click on different templates, and it shows you how they'll look. You see one you like, click the button, and it comes out all typeset in columns, with spaces for artwork and everything else.

Mark chose a simple letter format, eight pages long, and he did it all in one day. He thought to himself, "What if I sold 500 subscriptions at $100 each? Wow, wouldn't that be interesting?" Well, right away he sold 1,000 of them at $97. Boom, $97,000 came pouring in. By then, he'd only written a couple of issues -- about sixteen pages -- and most sales letters are longer than that. **In the end, he signed up more than 2,000 people and earned more than a quarter of a million dollars on that product he started in one day.**

That's one simple way to get started on a quick product. Now, the only drawback is, you have that commitment to fulfill; when you sell those subscriptions, you'll have to write the newsletter for the next full year. **But as I've said before, if**

it's something you're interested in, then it's fun and easy. The research is a tax write-off. If it's about golf, you get paid to study golf. If it's about fishing, you get paid to go to fishing spots that you want to go to anyway. If you're having trouble getting ideas for your newsletter, check out Jeff Gardner's book, *The Ultimate Million Dollar Idea Generator*. I've used Jeff Gardner's book myself to come up with fast ideas for titles we've needed for our products.

Keys to Self-Motivation

A deadline can be the entrepreneur's best friend. You need deadlines for all your great ideas because they're ideal motivators. You can sit and read this book and think, "Well, I'll do all these things one day," but then you'll be tempted to keep putting it off and putting it off. On the other hand, once you make a commitment, once you set some deadlines, it becomes increasingly easier to go ahead and get it done. **That's the whole thing: you have to take action.**

Here are some other motivational suggestions that will help you to create your product in one day. **First of all, why not create the ad first?** Before you even start on the actual one-day product, come up with the sales letter. Let's say your product is going to be called *Seven Ways to Make More Money with Your Website*. Your first task is to decide on all the greatest things you'd like to have in that product. Create a list of bullets and benefits. It's easy to come up with the first right answer, but the best material generally comes with the second, third, or fourth right answer. So if you say in your ad, "I'll tell you five ways to do this," the first one comes easy, and maybe the second one comes easy -- and then you have to think a while to get the next three. **What happens is, you create a better**

product because you've given yourself a goal to achieve. You force yourself to think it through and these points come to mind because you've given yourself the challenge. So you create a better product; you create a product with direction; you create a product that has more sales appeal built into it because you've created the ideal products first and then you have to work to live up to it.

Once you've got that list of answers, put them into your ad and get that ad out there in front of people where they can buy into it. Then it becomes very easy to do the product because you have a list of all of the things you told your customers or prospects they were going to be learning. I promise you: if you start with the ad first, you've got not just a powerful incentive to finish the product and get it out there, you've got a great way to sell a ton of products. Most people (including us, sometimes) do it the opposite way: they start with the product first. But that's turned out to be a serious mistake. **The times we've started with the ads first, we've made a ton of money**.

Another thing you can do to get yourself moving is to offer your customers a prepublication special. Even before the product comes out, you can tell your customers something like, "It's so new it's not even printed yet, but I'm going to make you a special deal that no one else gets. I'm going to give you this prepublication special price of 50% off." The customers love it. They want to be the first to get it and they like the fact that you're giving them a discount. Now you've created a deadline for yourself. You have to promise them that it'll be done and you have to give them a due date. Deadlines like these can really help to force you to move on things. When you do that you're more than halfway done and you're going to end up with a much more sellable product.

The Key Element to Selling Your Product

While you're creating, keep this in mind: in some cases, the advertisement or direct mail for your product is more important than the product itself. I know that sounds odd and you do need a good product, don't get me wrong. But the truth is, plenty of good products don't sell just because the advertising isn't right. When you start working with the advertising first, the sales letter, you're just doing the right thing; the bullet points and benefits in the advertising are what really sell your product.

Ted Nickel once said something in a seminar that absolutely knocked my socks off. He said he's written over 100,000 words of ad copy for his best selling manual, *How to Form Your Own Corporation*, over the years. Now, this best-selling book has sold about a million copies, but the manual itself consists of only about 35 or 40 pages. That's maybe 10,000 words, and yet he's written ten times that just in advertisements and sales letters. Why has he done that? "Because," he said, "<u>that's what sells the book and that's more important than the book itself</u>." That was quite a revelation.

Closer to home, Russ von Hoelscher, Eileen, and I once put together a very successful product called *The Millionaire Matrix*, which was an upgrade of an earlier product we did. We started with a list of the best benefits we could develop: the five best ways to do this, the six best ways to do that. Then we simply recorded eight audiocassette tapes around those

---

benefits. But be careful when doing this because it's so easy to get off track -- and for Pete's sake, don't be boring.

Use grandiose, exciting, and powerful words to describe your product. Make liberal use of buzz words and benefit words that'll hook people in. <u>There's nothing more important than the sales material and boring copy doesn't sell anything</u>. Always look for the hidden benefits, the excitement, the passion that's in your product, and then convey that in the words you put on the Internet or in your direct mail package.

Otherwise, who's going to buy? They say that if you build a better mousetrap, the world will beat a path to your door. **Well, that's not true if the world doesn't know you built the mousetrap**. Even then, you have to romance it a bit. When they first invented Pepsodent toothpaste, years ago, they couldn't give it away; nobody wanted to hear about how good it was at fighting gingivitis, though that was true. It was Claude Hopkins (who wrote Scientific Advertising) who came along and said, "Try this: 'If you brush your teeth with Pepsodent toothpaste, you'll have sex appeal.'" They did, and sales went through the roof.

It's all in how you present the product. Even when penicillin was first invented, it had to be sold. The scientists all went, "Well, that's exciting," and just kind of ignored it. No one really knows or cares what something will do unless you can explain it in a way they can grasp emotionally. You can't just give them the facts; you have to say, "Here's why penicillin is so great. Here's what it will do for you. It will change the world."

Be Yourself, Enjoy Yourself

One thing I'd like to reiterate is that almost everyone **can create these one-day products, especially the audio versions.** I honestly believe that. The secret is to get excited, to show your listener (or reader) that you care about them, and to be yourself. Don't try to pretend you're somebody you're not. People will respect you if they know you really want to help them. I feel that a lot of very successful people have funny accents -- like the ones like Eileen and I have because we're from the Midwest.

Even Dan Kennedy, a professional speaker who earns over $1,000,000 a year from the platform, has a stuttering problem he still has to deal with. **If you really, sincerely want to help other people, and just be yourself, that can transcend other weaknesses and limitations, whatever they may be.** That's why it also helps if you're doing a product about something you have a real natural interest and enthusiasm for; it just comes across in the presentation. You're more interested in the material than in what your voice sounds like.

As I've mentioned, one thing that helps many people who are a little self-conscious is to create a product from an interview situation. Prepare the questions and give them to a friend of yours whom you're comfortable with. Then the two of you sit down, they interview you by asking the questions that you've provided them, and you just naturally give your answers. That tends to relax most people. They're with someone they're already comfortable with, they're providing answers to questions they already know the answers to, and they get excited. **There's a level of interaction there that they're much more comfortable with than if they were speaking alone into a tape recorder. You can try to actually teach the interviewer verbally what you know and record it**

as you go.

Then there are panel discussions, which is how we create a lot of products here at M.O.R.E., Inc. For example, this book is based on a panel discussion with Alan Bechtold, Mark Nolan, Chris Lakey, Russ von Hoelscher, and the other folks I talked about in Chapter 1. <u>When a group of people in the same business get together and get excited, and everybody's pumped up about the information they're sharing, then the listener who buys the recordings or printed transcripts is drawn into the conversation</u>. It's very much like when you go to a party and see a small group of people in the corner and everybody's animated and laughing and waving their arms around. You just naturally want to go over to that corner to see what in the world these people are talking about.

Choose the Right Title!

Names are important; smart people have realized that for thousands of years. So it's very important is to give your products great titles. **Maybe you can't judge a book by its title, but you can certainly sell a book by its title**. There was a great publisher named E. Haldeman-Julius who published right out of Kansas, not far from where Eileen and I live. He publish hundreds of these little blue paperback books from the 1930s to the 1950s, and the big secret that he revealed in his book *The First Hundred Million* (in other words, he sold over a hundred million of his little books) was that he changed the titles constantly. It made a huge difference, especially when the original titles were a little dull.

One book he produced was originally called Casanova's Diary, and of course it was about the world famous lover.

Haldeman-Julius sold about 35,000 copies the first year. Then he changed the title to Diary of the World's Greatest Lover, and sold over a 100,000. **All it took was a more interesting title to sell three times as many copies**. That's a good example of why you want great headlines in all your ads and sales letters and great names for your information products, too.

You can also use a new title to re-purpose an existing book. Melvin Powers tells a story about how he found a rhyming dictionary in a used bookstore that was out of copyright. He took that dictionary and called it The Songwriters Rhyming Dictionary. There was no rhyming dictionary directed specifically to songwriters and it was a hit; he's sold it successfully for years and years.

Get into the Recording Habit

I want to re-emphasize, here, just how easy it is to produce audio recordings, especially if you just get in the habit of trying to record for 15 minutes a day. First it starts with a title, as I discussed earlier; you have to have a great title. If you're following the best of our strategies, you've also written some sales material, whether in a full-page ad, a flyer, or a sales letter, so you know exactly what you need to talk about. Go to Radio Shack; for a few hundred dollars you can find an excellent tape recorder to get started with, though it doesn't have to be that great. Or these days, just use your computer -- all you need is a good microphone or headset to record right onto your laptop and the quality tends to be very good.

Then all you do is spend about 20 to 30 minutes every day writing out your notes, so you cover exactly what you're going to talk about. After 20 to 30 minutes of thinking it all through in the morning while you're drinking your first cup of coffee, simply go and record for 15 minutes. Every three days you'll have a 45-minute cassette tape. By packaging them together, you can create those very expensive products I've mentioned. Just get in the habit. Fifteen minutes is nothing; after all, how long do you spend watching television?

I've discussed the fact that you can start a newsletter or similar product just by collecting newspaper clippings. Well, here's a great example of a guy who's doing just that, and making a huge amount of money: Randy Cassingham, who runs the website Thisistrue.com.

Basically it's "Ripley's Believe It or Not" type stuff, bizarre news stories that he collects from all the press services. He's got all those feeds that come in, and he looks through them and he finds funny headlines, really dumb headlines, or just bizarre stories that make you think, "How could people be that stupid?"

He rewrites them a bit and he puts them on his website, and will send them to you once a week if you send him fifteen bucks. Now, fifteen bucks for a whole year doesn't seem like much, but he has well over 100,000 subscribers. Now, add that up: the guy's making over a million dollars a year reading funny stories and rewriting them and making comments.

You can do that with any subject you're really interested in. That's key: you have got to really be interested in it, it's got to be something that you think is fun, and it's got to be something you're proud of and feel really serves people. Randy Cassingham is making everybody laugh; it makes your day to read his output, so it's a valuable service.

Trash or Treasure; or,
Learn to Believe in YOU

No matter what you choose to do, it has to represent something that's valuable to the market you're serving. And let me point out that it doesn't matter if it's junk to anyone else, as long as it's of value to your market. For example, years back we offered a collection of all of the greatest ads and sales letters from our company, from Russ von Hoelscher, and from a lot of other folks we work with on a regular basis. We came up with a huge product and probably two-thirds of it was the actual ads and sales letters we used to do business. We didn't have to typeset them, we didn't have to do anything; the material was already put together. Yes, it was easy to put together, but it represented value to our customers. That's the point, the secret of creating something that the rest of the world can think of as junk. Who cares what they think? **You won't be making everyone happy.** You can't.

As long as your customers value it, then other people's trash is your customer's treasure. It's that simple.

But it's hard for people to believe that. One of the questions we marketers get asked all the time by our clients is, "Why would anybody be interested in what I know?" They're insecure; they find it so hard to believe that they know enough about anything that someone else would want to listen to them. **What you've got to realize (and you never notice until you really start doing this) is that there's always someone who doesn't know as much about a given subject that you're interested in as you do, at whatever**

---

level. Sure, there are always people who know more than you, but there are also always going to be people who know less than you.

The ones that know less than you and want to know what you know are your customers! I call it "the diminished I" syndrome. People think to themselves, "If I know it, it can't be valuable. Everyone else must also know it." But, generally, that's just not the truth. While there are some people running around who don't know very much and pretend to know it all, most people are self-deprecating -- despite the fact that they're better than they ever thought that they were.

Dare to Be Daring

There's a place in the Bible where Jesus says that no man is a prophet in his own home; nobody wants to listen to you.
Every consultant knows you've got to go to some other city, and you've got to be coming off of an airplane, before anybody's going to pay you $1,000 an hour. And when you get there, you've also got to be daring and audacious.

Consider the man who invented the Soloflex exercise system, Jerry Wilson -- this guy is a multi-millionaire entrepreneur right now, but he used to be a professional pilot, flying a corporate plane from L.A. to Las Vegas and back. All of his clients were high-rolling Beverly Hills movie stars and millionaires. Wilson got to know these people personally over a decade or so while they were flying. By then, he's about 55 years old and the gray is setting in. One morning he just looks in the mirror and asks himself, "What is it that these people have that I don't have?"

He decided that there was only one thing, and one thing only, that all those multi-millionaires had. It was audacity. They were audacious people. **They weren't waiting for other people to discover them; they were out there making things happen well before they were ever discovered.** Some of these people were twenty-year "overnight success" stories because they'd worked hard behind the scene promoting themselves. **You can't be self-deprecating if you want to make money hand-over-fist.** That's what this pilot learned from his regular passengers.

A small plane like a Learjet is an intimate setting. You're kind of chummy. These people would knock back a few drinks while Jerry Wilson was flying and they'd start to talk. He'd listen to their stories and say to himself, "I can't believe this. This is audacious. I just can't believe this guy." He'd tell his wife and, finally, she was the one who said, "Maybe you need to be audacious for once." **The point is, instead of being such a straight, reliable, boring person, do something crazy; nothing that would hurt anyone, but get wild.** Be bold. Take action. Boldness has genius, power, and magic in it.

I think that Jerry Wilson's story presents both an excellent example and an excellent challenge for anybody interested in making money, because the facts are all there in public sources, in most cases. You can read great biographies -- and sometimes autobiographies -- about all these people, like Jerry Wilson and Bill Gates and Michael Dell, who've made lots of money. Well, you know what?

When it all comes down to it, they -- we -- are no different than you. The only thing that we have is we did it.

We got started somewhere.

We started with a plan of action...well, actually, many of us probably started with no plan of action. **That's something that I want to reiterate: just DO SOMETHING!**

If you don't have a customer base, if you don't have a product, use one of the ideas I've presented here to acquire them. **Start by reading this entire book again, at least once.** Pick one idea that you can turn into a product. Start there. If you've got a customer base, you're better off than a lot of people. You can easily turn one of these products into thousands of dollars within a few days.

Just get started! Practice these ideas. As Joe Cossman, the famous millionaire, once said, "Everything is difficult before it becomes easy." I used to think Joe was such an amazing genius for coming up with that idea -- then I discovered that Aristotle had said the same thing two thousand years ago. This is an idea that's timeless. **Everything that is difficult becomes easy. The more you do something, the easier it becomes.**

Be bold! Be audacious!

Get out there and make things happen. Get some customers and then start developing informational products for those customers. Remember, it all becomes so much easier once you have people who've bought from you, who trust you, and want to buy from you again and again. <u>Even when you invent a product in one day, it can make you money for many, many years.</u>

So get started now and start getting rich with your own fast informational products!

www.ingramcontent.com/pod-product-compliance
Lightning Source LLC
Chambersburg PA
CBHW032015190326
41520CB00007B/491